How

Be Motivated

Achieve Unstoppable Motivation and Positivity in Your Daily Life While Making Sure It Stays That Way so That You Can Beat Procrastination and Achieve Success in All Areas of Life

By Clark Darsey

Contents

Thank you for buying this book and I hope that you will find it useful. If you will want to share your thoughts on this book, you can do so by leaving a review on the Amazon page, it helps me out a lot.

Introduction

Motivation is important. It is the reason individuals prosper and the reason individuals fall short. Motivation is the drive somebody has to accomplish a task. The motivation ingredients are mixed with lots of elements that include simplicity, attitude, individuals you hang around, how you think, understanding yourself, assisting other individuals and so a lot more.

The aim of this guide is to take you through techniques you could practice every day to stay motivated. These methods can assist you in feeling better about yourself in all you do. You could take these techniques with you when you head to work and when you are at home.

Motivation is the fire everybody requires to make it through the day, to set and meet targets, and more. Without motivation, you are going to fail. When you are apathetic towards something, you are not motivated since you could not care either way. This is the lousiest mindset you could have due to the fact that it isn't negative either. Somebody who feels this way isn't capable of accomplishing anything since they don't care if they do or not. In case you are feeling like this, this guide is precisely what you require to help you conquer your mindset and start feeling motivated once again.

When you understand how to stay motivated by yourself, you could additionally aid others since your mindset is going to be contagious. When you practice everyday motivational methods, ultimately, they are going to come to you naturally. Initially, a few of these techniques might be tough for you to do or to keep in mind. It is going to require time for you to start to practice and follow these methods naturally.

Chapter 1: Make It Simple

When considering motivation, the initial thing you want to do is to make the space around you at home and work. This space has to stay positive and simple. The things around you have a great deal to do with how you feel and if you are going to be inspired or stuck in a funk.

Your office space ought to consist of and display things which make you feel favorable about attaining goals and life in general. If you have goals and things you want to do, it may be a great idea to place these things on the wall of your cubicle or your office. By doing this, you have a continuous reminder of the important things you would ultimately like to do.

Only you understand where you wish to be in the future. You ought to design your space as a continuous and positive reminder that you are working on getting there. Make a favorable atmosphere around you regardless of where you are.

This additionally consists of the vehicle you drive. If you spend numerous hours in the vehicle driving each day, make it a positive space. This indicates to clean it up. Do not drive around a dismal car that is full of garbage and paperwork. Get your vehicle detailed and start to look after it. You would be shocked how excellent you are going to feel when you clean up your vehicle.

A tidy home and tidy workplace make a truly big deal when you require motivation. If you end up being in mounds of paperwork, you may have the mindset that you will never finish the things you have to do. An untidy workspace could be discouraging and depressing. It might cause you to put things off and even be disordered with your thoughts in addition to your work.

An untidy and filthy home could be disabling and depressing. A lot of individuals are going to sit around putting things off for hours in an untidy home. It is remarkable how great a tidy home could make you feel. The ideal thing you can do is tidy up your home. You are going to feel terrific and all set to take on anything. Throw away the clothes that have actually been sitting in the closet for years which you have not worn once. Clear out the mess in the garage and the shed. Do not simply do the dishes and wipe down the counters. A tidy home implies developing a brand-new space which is positive and all set for new things to come into your home. Do away with all of the old.

The space you spend your time in entails your vehicle, home, and the workplace you work in. It has a great deal to do with how you feel and the mindset you have when you get up in the morning. Tidy up the areas you reside in and make a favorable atmosphere for you to delight in. You are going to then see the goals as possible instead of sitting around thinking about them.

Chapter 2: Maintaining Excellent Company

Socializing with positive individuals is among the ideal ways to be inspired. You ought to speak to somebody positive at least one time a day. A number of the ways you could have a positive encounter with individuals consist of face to face, over the phone, and over the computer. Try to make this a daily habit.

Certain individuals are not really social. They may go days without speaking with others. This is really unhealthy. If you are among these individuals who are not really social, and you find that you do not have lots of encounters with other people, you most likely additionally are not too inspired to be successful additionally. This does not indicate you need to be a social bug. What this implies is that you want to feed your requirement for positive interaction. You do not need to see the other individual either. There are methods you could practice to encounter others positively without even seeing them personally. How you do these things is up to you, yet this is really essential.

Maintaining an excellent company indicates socializing with others who are encouraging you and your goals in life. You wish for individuals to support you and have faith in you as well. In case you have goals to be successful with your own gardening business, you ought to socialize with individuals who are encouraging. If you are around individuals who are negative about your ventures and unsupportive, you are not going to feel great about it whatsoever. Get rid of the negativity. If these individuals are family members, it may be the hardest decision you ever made. Nevertheless, it is going to be the ideal thing you could do for you. If individuals are not encouraging or positive, then cut them out.

The most typical way you could have an encounter with somebody daily is to speak to individuals. You ought to have routine encounters with positive individuals. The ideal method to begin your day is to have coffee each morning with a positive individual. If you live close to your buddy who is a coffee drinker, then you could plan to leave for work sooner each day and have coffee at their house or have them drop by. This is an outstanding method to begin your day and place you in a terrific state of mind for work. You are going to already have started your day socially, so when you get to work, you will not feel like such a grouch.

In case you do not have time in the mornings to meet with somebody or any other time of day you ought to look for the time to speak to somebody on the phone. You may have a buddy you could call and speak to or a member of the family. Make sure the individual is somebody who makes you feel excellent about life and yourself.

In case you do not like to speak on the phone and you do not have time to come by and speak to somebody each day, then you may consider the web as your finest option. Many individuals utilize this technique as a means to keep an excellent company. When you are online, you could join a chatroom for almost anything nowadays. There are plenty of chatrooms all across the web. Make sure to select a chat room which has to do with something you feel excellent about. For example, if you have a goal to do something, you may join a group with others who are pursuing the identical goal. This is a great way to increase your positive mindset and inspire you to pursue that goal.

Negativity could nearly be contagious in certain scenarios. You wish to make certain individuals you are speaking to are positive. If the individual you pick to socialize with is a negative individual who is constantly grumbling and who sees the negative in all the things, they may not be who you wish to help you end up being inspired. Negativity is going to just bring you down and induce you to be negative as well.

Chapter 3: Constant Learning

Learning promotes development. It is good for the brain and you are never ever too old to find out new things. Each day you ought to attempt to learn something brand-new. The ideal way to accomplish this is via listening and reading.

If you are typically not inspired to start new tasks or to take on brand-new things, you ought to boost your learning. You do not need to be a devoted reader and take on novels, yet you ought to read. Reading benefits the brain and it is stimulating for the mind. Constantly learning brand-new things is going to aid you to become open to handling things you didn't believe you could do prior.

A morning newspaper is a typical method certain individuals like to stimulate their brains. They may like to snuggle up with the paper and their coffee prior to starting their long day. You can also read the newspaper each night prior to going to sleep. This is an outstanding habit to get into.

Reading the newspaper could be tough for certain individuals. You may not like the newspaper due to the ink, or you may believe in recycling, and you may be against the abundance of newspapers being printed. You do not need to read the newspaper. You could check out the news online daily at your computer. You do not need to be on a news website yet you could read anything which interests you. Perhaps you wish to discover a brand-new skill. You could go to a website that concentrates on this skill and read a bit each day.

Reading is not the sole activity you might do to be learning continually. If you do not have time to read or if you do not enjoy reading, there are other ways you may learn. Lots of folks who have long commutes frequently listen to audiobooks. Certain individuals get to know a different language or listen to a novel. There are various things you may listen to at any time of day.

Listening could additionally include your tv while you are preparing for work. You may select to switch on the news and listen to the news each morning. You could listen to public radio or a cooking channel. You do not need to read if you are not a huge reader.

Listening to your buddies, family and other individuals is another crucial aspect you want to concentrate on to stay inspired. When you listen to others, they are going to wish to be around you since they are going to know what they say means something to you and you are going to learn. You are going to feel excellent about yourself as you respect others, which is going to create motivation.

Constant learning is exceptionally crucial to motivation. Each day you ought to have a routine of learning something. You may wish to read the newspaper every day, listen to the radio or tapes, or perhaps simply listen to individuals.

Chapter 4: The Power of Positive Thinking

Positive thinking is crucial to your whole way of life. If you wish to attain a goal, you need to be positive. Positive thinking can be attained in numerous ways, and it is what is going to aid you in ending up being motivated to do things. If you are negative about accomplishing a goal, you are going to put things off and not wish to work toward the goal. There are numerous ways to have a positive mindset.

Concentrate on the Crucial Things

It is extremely common for individuals to focus their energy on things which are trivial. When your emotional energy is devoted towards things which are trivial, it could be extremely draining. The initial thing you want to do is to be extremely clear about the things in your life which are essential to you. Make a vision and mission for your goals and your life. These things are essential to you. In this manner, when you end up being upset about something, you could take a step back when you get aggravated and choose if it actually deserves the energy or not. Most of the times, you are going to find that you are squandering energy and becoming upset about particular scenarios and things which you should not be upset about. This could be unhealthy and is extremely bad. When you are clear about the essential things, you are going to maintain a positive mindset, and you are not going to get distressed as much.

Maintain Good Health

Motivation additionally means you need to be a healthy individual. It's not possible to have a positive mindset when you do not look after your body. There are 3 main things you want to do so as to build a healthy body. These things involve eating properly, getting ample exercise and sleeping.

Your diet plan could have a great deal to do with the manner in which you feel daily. A well-balanced diet plan could make you feel excellent each day and positive. If you drink a lot of soda, you may develop a caffeine dependency that creates headaches. This could addionally lead to you not having the motivation to do anything either.

Eating a healthy and balanced diet plan implies cutting out sugars, fatty foods, alcohol, and other things which get you down. A well-balanced diet could assist you in dropping weight as well. Being overweight could be a variable which causes you to be dissatisfied with yourself and have a negative outlook. The ideal diet plan has lots of fruits, veggies, chicken and fish, and a great deal of water. Watch your serving sizes as well. If you are consuming the appropriate foods, you may simply have to reduce the portion sizes you consume.

Exercise is additionally essential to have a great mindset. Everybody ought to exercise daily. You ought to take at least 15 minutes each day to exercise. You do not need to do aerobics or something too exhausting. Walking is the ideal thing you may do for your body. A vigorous 15-minute walk each day is going to make you feel excellent and totally alter your mindset. This is going to additionally make you inspired and create a positive mindset about the directions you could go in.

If you are somebody who is confined to a desk for a big chunk of your day and you do not think you have time to work out that is simply an excuse. There are desk exercises you may do as you are sitting. Throughout your lunch hour, you may pick to walk around the outside of the building or perhaps in the corridors of the interior of the building as well. The stairs at your walk might lead to an exceptional workout too.

Share

One more thing you may do to create a positive mindset is to give. Giving implies not just presents but your time, energy and attention. You may give yourself by hanging around with individuals who require it. Hang out with a friend in the hospital or do something to improve somebody's mindset. Among the very best ways to improve your mindset and feel fantastic is by giving to individuals.

You may give presents, yet you do not need to spend cash. It is truly easy to take five minutes out of your day to do something great for somebody else.

Additionally, it is frequent to stumble upon scenarios which are the ideal chance for you to step in and assist out. Many times individuals are stuck on the side of the road with a broken-down car and nobody stops to aid them like they used to. Individuals simply drive by and assume the individual has a mobile phone. Help may imply giving somebody the fifty cents when they are short at the checkout or helping the neighbor with constructing a fence.

Get Rid of Unneeded Items

In case your home is jumbled with things you do not require or which are simply using up space. You may think about giving those things away. The old saying that 'another person's junk is another's treasure' truly does ring true. You may be so concentrated on belongings and the important things that you own which you actually do not take pleasure in life as you ought to. Maybe you grew up without anything, and that is why possessions are so essential to you. One of the ideal ways to feel excellent about yourself and offer yourself a quick boost is to give. When you recognize that those possessions you own actually aren't that vital to you and give them away, that is an exceptional boost. You are going to feel extremely excellent about yourself.

Take a **Look at the Interesting Side**

Life is interesting. When you see the interesting part of life and the humor in stuff, you are going to have an exceptional mindset. You are going to find that individuals who have the very best mindset frequently have the funniest sense of humor. When you have a great sense of humor, you are going to feel excellent about life and be positive as well. A positive mind is somebody who sees the good in things and in even the small stuff. This could additionally aid you to generate motivation so you could proceed and attain the objectives you are going to set.

If you are somebody who has a tendency to be serious at almost everything, you may wish to step back and notice the funny side of things. Being too serious could just result in stress and concern. When you are stressed out and anxious, you are additionally concentrating on negative things.

Concentrate on the positive and the funny. For the most part, you may be able to discover something funny about the majority of things.

Concentrate on Your Strengths

Everybody has strengths, and they are proficient at something. You may be among the countless individuals who are working a job which does you no justice. You may have qualifications far and beyond what you are doing daily. This is an objective you could set for yourself to utilize your strengths. Nevertheless, daily, you could practice the things you delight in and the things you are proficient at. If you do not have the time to do these things each day, you ought to put time aside to do these things at least 3 times a week or perhaps during the weekend.

When you concentrate on things you are proficient at, that makes you feel excellent. You ought to have a pastime if you are not able to do these things as you are working each day. If you like crafts and arts or composing, you ought to spend the time doing these things. This could aid you end up being positive. When you concentrate on strengths and things you enjoy, you are going to additionally end up being motivated to attain goals focused around these things. This may entail going into a contest or making an application for a job.

The ideal thing you may do for yourself is using your strengths. Consider the things that you delight in doing. Consider the things you are proficient at. You know you are good at something. You ought to think about these things and start to concentrate on them. Set time aside for yourself to take pleasure in these things. Make certain you concentrate on something which makes you feel excellent. If you are bad at this task it is still fine. You may be the worst painter, yet if it makes you feel great and positive, then you ought to continue. Disregard any negativity which comes your way throughout this time too.

One final point, when you pick things to do which make you feel excellent, make certain these things are healthy. If you feel excellent when you drink wine since you forget about the bad, it might create an issue. Select a skill or anything positive for you which makes you feel excellent.

Create **Buffers**

Buffers are essential in your life. As you go through life, you are going to discover there are particular scenarios that you have no control of. A lot of things through life are beyond your control. You should not try to manage anybody or have too much control over the things which occur in your life. Your positive mindset is going to aid you handle your life and the things you do. You want to produce buffers so that you accept the reality that you do not have control over the scenario.

When you make buffers, you may select to speak to buddies to work you through particular situations. You may select to speak to a therapist or a counselor to make it through a difficult time. Lots of folks practice meditation to aid them accept they do not have control over the realities dealt with during the days. You may wish to create an external support group, so when the bad does strike, you have individuals to help you through the tough times.

Chapter 5: Procrastination

Procrastination could be why you do not make it through lots of tasks during the day. You may discover you get drawn into a tv show or playing on the web. When you take a look at the clock, the day has passed, and you have not finished any of your work. This absence of productivity is going to cause you to be really uninspired.

Procrastination could be detrimental. The impacts could additionally be damaging if your procrastination leads to issues with your work life, private life and more. Putting things off is a major issue for many individuals.

Lots of people are really mindful of the fact they put things off, yet they can not leave the funk they are stuck in. You can. It is prevalent to stand around and think about how things might be or how things are going to be. You may have a task you have to finish and sit around and consider doing the task but never get going with it. You may meet deadlines at the final minute. This does not make anybody feel great about themselves.

If your motivation is missing on a task, you may think about shifting the focus to something else which has to get done. In case you have a paper due and you can not get focused, do not sit before the computer system and play around. Discover something else around your home to do, and after that, go back to get the paper done. Beginning another task might provide you with the momentum you require to get going with the task you have to get done.

Procrastination could be really destructive. You may be mindful or unaware of the procrastination you deal with. Nevertheless, you want to focus on the time you spend sitting around not doing anything. When you are able to conquer procrastination, and you end up being completely productive, you are going to be extremely positive about life. You are going to additionally be inspired to handle new projects as well, since you are going to be spending less time lingering.

Chapter 6: Understanding Yourself

One of the ways you may work on an everyday basis to motivate yourself is to learn more about yourself. You want to concentrate on yourself and consider the important things which make you feel great and the important things which make you feel lousy.

Writing is an extremely healthy way to learn more about you. You may wish to attempt writing in a journal or utilizing lists. Lists could be really valuable for ending up being positive and learning more about you. Initially, make a list of the important things which you feel great about. These may be from the initial cup of coffee in the morning, or reaching a huge goal.

Write a list of all of the important things which you take pleasure in doing and the things which you enjoy. This list could aid you in creating a positive environment by surrounding yourself with positive things in your life. This list is going to additionally aid you to produce better and more positive days.

You are going to feel inspired to create a life loaded with positive things which make you delighted.

You ought to additionally write about the things which are negative in your life and the important things which trouble you. This list ought to consist of everything which may induce you to feel negative about days or occasions in your life. They may affect you somehow. You may have a chair in your living room you completely dislike. Place it on your list of things to get rid of it.

As soon as you have the negative list assembled, you want to start making certain these items and habits are taken out of your life. Think about the ways in which you could create your days around just the positive things free from the negativity.

When you learn more about yourself, it is the ideal thing you may do. It is necessary to comprehend the things which make you feel positive and the things which bring negative feelings to you. The better you are able to create your life in a positive fashion, you are going to be completely inspired to live it completely.

Chapter 7:Setting Goals and Tracking Progress

Goal setting is the most crucial thing. If you do not have any goals, you must be quite bored. Certain individuals sit around each day and say they are content with going back and forth to work to the identical job each and every single day, every year. You see nothing taking place, and you can constantly guess where they are going to be since they never do a thing beyond their routine. You may be among these individuals.

Setting goals assists you to grow. It makes you feel great to set goals and pursue making them happen. Goal setting is healthy for your mind and body. Among the important things to think about when it pertains to setting goals is that you do not wish to sit around and speak about the goals you have. This is going to do you no good and it will only discourage you.

When you set goals they need to be reasonable and obtainable or you are going to be discouraged.

Always set goals which you actually are able to reach, and for which you see how to meet them. It is essential to jot down the actions it is going to require to achieve the goal. Choose how long it is going to take you to achieve every task. This may be in days or weeks. As soon as you do this, you are going to want to set a date when you are going to start pursuing the goal. Then you could set the project up on a calendar and jot down where you need to be with every activity.

As you start a project or a completion of a goal, you need to track the progression. As you meet specific milestones, you want to treat yourself to something special due to the fact that you are one action closer to doing something you feel is necessary. If you are running behind, you may want to pick it up a notch or extend out the deadline. Make sure that you are just running behind because you underestimated how long things are going to take.

Goal setting is extremely crucial. When you establish goals and lay them out with milestones and time frames, you are going to be more inspired to finish them. As you attain specific milestones, you are going to be motivated more than ever to reach the completion of the task. This is an extremely positive way to work on projects, specifically if you have a difficult time finishing them.

Chapter 8: Assisting Others

Assisting others is extremely crucial to make yourself feel excellent and feel positive about your life. When you aid others, you are going to feel really motivated with your life. Much of the ways you can assist others consist of sharing knowledge, visiting others, aiding individuals to see positive, and a lot more.

Sharing your knowledge is a great idea. There is a distinction in between sharing your knowledge with individuals rather than your viewpoint. If you have anything to say which is valuable and informative, then it is a good idea. Make certain you are clear about offering your viewpoint. This is going to just make you feel bad later on if you hurt somebody's feelings.

Knowledge sharing implies you speak about the things you understand. If you are informed or competent on a particular subject perhaps you could offer to teach individuals how to do the things you understand. If you are a proficient underwater basket weaver, then share what you know. There are always individuals who are delighted to discover something brand-new. It is going to, in fact, make you feel excellent to share your knowledge with other people.

Spend Time with Buddies

It is really common for individuals to be negative and have an attitude problem. If you know one of these individuals, you do not wish to spend a lot of time socializing with them or looking for a positive experience, or you may find yourself ending up being negative as well. Among the things you may do is to aid these individuals in producing a more positive mindset towards life and their natural surroundings.

Certain individuals are so negative they are really difficult to be around. It might be aggravating. As you use your motivational methods daily, you may find it difficult to be around them. This is where you could make an effort to aid these individuals.

Nevertheless, do not make this job so tough that you end up being annoyed.

When you assist negative individuals by hanging out with them, it does not imply you will transform their mindset. Your positive mindset could be contagious. When somebody is feeling negative or down in the dumps, you could aid them by seeing the positive side of the scenario. You could aid them see the excellent in the negative things which are occurring in their lives. You could additionally aid them understand that they have no control over the circumstances. The quicker somebody recognizes they have no complete control over issues in their life, they are going to have the ability to let it go and unwind.

Hanging out with negative buddies indicates sharing your positive mindset. You wish to share this energy yet do not force it upon anybody. Do not try too much to alter somebody.

Discover the Good in Other Individuals

Everybody does have a good side even if you do not see it straight away upon meeting them. Certain individuals may strike you as completely negative. Immediately upon meeting somebody, the initial encounter might be unfriendly and aggravating. Look for the positive side in individuals regardless of how tough they appear to be.

When you are around negative individuals, they are going to have a negative effect on you. It is necessary to make an effort and find the good in others. Everybody has good things. The more good you discover in others, the simpler it is going to be to speak to them and be around them. In case you are forced to be around negative individuals in a meeting or certain other scenario you can not avoid, discovering the positive is going to aid you make it through them.

Being More Positive with Everybody

Despite the fact that you are trying to find the positive facets in negative individuals, you want to stay positive in all the things you do. Be positive with individuals you are around every day. The more positive you are to individuals, the more inspired you are going to feel as well.

You do not need to suck up to anybody when you are positive. If you are around individuals you do not like, you still do not need to be negative. You could be a positive individual and discover the great in all the things. The coffee may taste fantastic and you slept well. If you didn't manage to beat the traffic, then at least you had a terrific audio to listen to on your way to work.

It is about concentrating on the small things and discovering the positive in them. The more positivity you discover in individuals and the things around you, the happier you are going to be. You are going to additionally be more inspired to make it through each day and hit your goals.

Transmit Your Positive Mindset

You may feel terrific and positive. Make certain to transmit your mindset to others around you and when you are indirectly speaking to individuals too. A positive mindset is addictive, and individuals are going to take pleasure in hanging out around you. They are going to feel excellent too. This could aid you in moving up in the business world as well.

When you have a positive mindset, you want to transmit it to other people. This additionally includes when you are on the computer or on the phone. It is common for a communication disconnect to happen when you are on the phone. You may be exhausted or not even notice to the other individual you are coming off impolite. Transmit your positive mindset to others when you speak to them on the phone. This is good for you, and it is going to make the other individual feel great about you.

Let Individuals Know You Care

Among the ways you could be more inspired and feel terrific about yourself daily is to let individuals understand that you care. Much like the little things in life that you take pleasure in so much, it is about the little things you can do to make others feel excellent as well. You do not need to get credit for these things. You are going to feel excellent making another person feel great. Often you are going to feel even better doing things for individuals without them recognizing who it is.

When you do things for other people, it could be a variety of things. You may consider sending out token items to loved ones such as flowers and cards. Anybody you appreciate, you ought to constantly let them know that you care. You do not need to purchase items and spend cash. If you do not have the cash to spend, there are other ways to do great things for individuals. These things may include something uncomplicated such as pouring them a cup of coffee, cleaning their vehicle, or something else.

Allowing individuals know you appreciate them is essential to them, yet it also is going to make you feel excellent. You ought to constantly let individuals know that you care and you value them. There are many ways in which you could allow individuals know that you care, and you do not need to spend cash either.

Share Your Sense of Humor

Laughing is good for your mind and body. If you know certain funny jokes or you start to see the funny part of life, you ought to share this with your buddies and individuals you are around. A sense of humor is great for you and it is good for other individuals too. The capability to make individuals laugh is a great thing and if you can make individuals laugh, utilize this ability. This is going to benefit individuals you are making laugh since you are raising their spirits, and it is going feel great to you as well.

Sharing your sense of humor benefits you and individuals you are around. You are going to feel great about yourself and may even be inspired to find brand-new jokes for every day as well.

Be a Great Listener

Aiding others to create motivation and a positive mindset additionally implies that you want to be a great listener. When you listen to individuals, they recognize that you, in fact, appreciate what they have to say. It reveals that you have a delicate side as well.

Listening to individuals offers you the chance to reveal to the individuals the positive in then negative they are concentrating on. This is going to help you help them. Listening implies comprehending how the individual is feeling about what they are saying. You may wish to repeat back to the individual a few of the things they are saying. This is going to reinforce to the individual you are listening to that you are listening to them. When you are an excellent listener, it is going to make you feel fantastic due to the fact that you are going to see the positive impact it has on the other individual. You are going to additionally get a better buddy too.

Offer Your Positive Mindset

There are lots of ways you may offer a positive mindset to other individuals. Some ways involve laughing, giving compliments, and setting an example.

Laughing is contagious. Individuals are frequently drawn to laughter, and they wish to take part in the fun. Laughing is additionally healthy as well. You may discover that individuals who frequently laugh actually are healthy and happy people. You ought to share your laugh and your mindset is going to be really contagious to individuals around you. You are going to feel excellent about yourself too.

Communicating your positive mindset could be done with a positive mindset and the ideal way to communicate that is through paying compliments to individuals. When you see the positive side in others constantly, feel free to share this with them. Notice somebody's great shoes or hat. Individuals enjoy compliments, and it gives them a boost, and is going to make you feel great about yourself additionally.

One more way to give your positive mindset to other individuals is by setting an example. When you do good things and individuals around you see it they additionally are going to jump in and assist as well. This involves stopping along the side of the road and assisting somebody in changing a tire on the vehicle. You may see somebody at work in a break room tidying up a mess from a luncheon. When you offer your favorable mindset, and you aren't scared to give to others, individuals are going to join in.

There are numerous things which you may do to aid others. When you aid others with your positive mindset and habits it is going to feel fantastic. You are going to be inspired to aid others. By following these various methods, you are going to discover that you are far more motivated every day to complete specific tasks and you are going to be producing an environment which is positive.

Chapter 9: Building Motivational Habits

There are lots of ways you could develop motivational habits daily. Habits could be difficult to develop, but once you start working hard to meet them, they are going to start to come naturally to you. There are numerous things you may do to develop habits which are inspiring and positive.

Visual Motivators

Visual motivators are essential since your surroundings could produce the attitude you have each day. If you are in a negative environment, you will not feel inspired to do much whatsoever. One thing you may do is utilize visual motivators to develop a positive environment that will aid you every day.

Visual motivators are things which include favorable quotes for you to read and concentrate on. They may consist of a change you wish to make in your life. There are lots of posters you may select from to post on your walls. By doing this, you could concentrate on the positive.

If you do not wish to paste these things on your walls, you may think about a motivational calendar. Every day the calendar is going to offer you a brand-new quote for the day. Certain individuals like to utilize jokes and cartoons to keep a great mindset.

There are numerous things you may consider to be a visual motivator. These things consist of anything which makes you feel actually excellent and positive. Bear in mind which visual motivators are to be utilized to inspire you daily since they are going to be somewhere where you are going to see them each day.

Keep Positive Buddies

Buddies are individuals you get along with and individuals who appreciate you. Those individuals are going to always build you up and make you feel excellent.

If you have a pal who shoots you down or makes you feel bad constantly, then you should not keep them as a buddy. Constantly spend time with individuals who make you feel excellent about life and great about yourself. The more time you spend around individuals who make you feel excellent, the better you are going to feel.

It holds true that you end up being the people you hang out with. If individuals you hang out with just put you down and do not support the things that are crucial to you, it is going to be too difficult for you to end up being the motivated individual you wish to be. You want a positive support group.

If you choose to cut individuals out of your life who are not positive or assist you, it may be challenging for you. You may choose to slowly stop speaking to them, or you may try and speak to them about the negativity. If their friendship means a great deal to you, perhaps you could mention the negativity and see how they react.Certain individuals do not understand they are so negative up until somebody points it out. This might save a relationship, and perhaps you might have a partner to start the quest for motivation together.

Read and Listen

Listening and reading are 2 habits you need to develop for your day-to-day motivational routine. Reading is the ideal thing you may do to bolster your mind and develop self-confidence. So as to end up being the individual you aim to be, you need to read about how to be this person. You want to associate with individuals you appreciate and wish to be like to form these habits. It is really common that you end up being a mix of individuals you associate with since you pick up the habits. By now, we all know about that famous self-help concept of you being the average of the 5 people you hang around.

Self Talk

Positive self-talk is a really crucial everyday habit you want to develop. There are going to be scenarios you want to walk yourself through and positive talk is going to assist you in making it through these times. Self-talk could assist you in numerous ways. It could help you feel great about yourself and how you look and how you will perform on a particular occasion.

If you have a meeting, you are really worried about due to the fact that you need to give a presentation, positive self-talk could aid with encouraging yourself to do a great job. It isn't insane to talk yourself through scenarios.

As you would feed off of positive reinforcement through others, you could make that happen by yourself too. When you wake up in the morning and you want to offer yourself a little encouragement, there is absolutely nothing wrong with speaking to yourself about making it through the day. Produce positive situations in your head and make them take place. When you speak to yourself favorably, you are going to start to believe that and act positively.

Maintain a Positive Mindset

You must stay positive. Life is difficult and you have to get accustomed to it. As quickly as you stop believing life is so challenging, you are going to find that it ends up being a lot simpler. Do not concentrate on how hard life is. Deal with the troubles of life.

A positive mindset is essential to make it through your days and be inspired. When you are positive about particular occasions and situations that you typically consider too difficult, you are going to make it through the obstacles a lot easier.

The most crucial thing you want to keep in mind about your mindset is that when you recognize you can not choose and manage the situations. You do have complete control over the mindset towards scenarios you deal with. You could keep a positive mindset. A positive mindset is going to help you feel a lot better about particular scenarios as you encounter them, and they will not feel so tough.

Breaks

One of the important things to bear in mind is that you want to slow down from time to time and take a break. Provide yourself the time to refill the energy and charge your batteries. Taking a break suggests offering yourself a moment to unwind. This does not imply to get caught up in a world of procrastination. If you have a bad habit of getting sucked into tv, then do not take a break before the TV. Make sure the break you take is a short while not leading to an issue.

If you have a huge family and the house is typically disorderly, the 'me' time is really essential. The odds are good you need to wait up until all of the kids are asleep or early in the morning before they wake up. If you need to arrange this time for yourself, you ought to. You are going to marvel at how a bit of time to yourself every day is going to aid you to feel more inspired to deal with circumstances.

Share with Others

As soon as you have actually ended up being motivated, you could start to share your motivation with other people. When you share motivation, it is going to be infectious, and so will your enthusiasm. As you share your passions, you are going to additionally discover that you are now driven to brand-new heights of achievements and goals.

Make certain to share your motivation daily. This part of your day-to-day routine of motivation might not be something you do immediately due to the fact that you want to work on you initially.

Chapter 10: Making The Most Of Motivation

As you end up being motivated, there are particular methods you could additionally utilize daily for yourself to make the most of the motivation and make you feel excellent. A number of the things you want to think about consist of repercussions, enjoyment, directions, rewards and more.

Repercussions are consider of when it pertains to optimizing your motivation. You can think about the repercussions and even point them out if you are attempting to inspire other people for a great performance. It is necessary to keep in mind not to utilize repercussions as threats. Threats are going to induce individuals to be turned against you. There is a huge distinction between threats and awareness. For self-motivation, understanding the repercussions could aid somebody get their act together.

Rewards and incentives are extremely crucial. You may never treat yourself to something excellent, and it is time you did. Self-reward is among the ideal ways to get inspired. Go purchase that brand-new watch you have actually had your eyes on for a long time. Make certain it is after you attain that goal you are pursuing.

Directions are additionally a crucial way to get most out of your motivational strategies. You may discover that you can never ever depend on anybody since they constantly let you down. Possibly they didn't comprehend. Directions ought to be clear and detailed. Do not make somebody feel like a kid, but you can offer directions to aid individuals to make it through an expectation.

Many people work much better when they understand what you expect from them. You may have to jot down directions for yourself additionally. Never ever take on a project if you are uncertain about how to finish it. If there are concerns about the actions included, always make certain to ask questions. Clarity on particular projects is going to aid you end up being more motivated to make it to the completion date.

Set goals for your action process. These goals ought to be long term and short term. Be clear on which objectives are reasonably obtainable in a short-term time frame and which objectives might take years to attain. Goals could help you direct the process of action and assist you in developing beliefs in your life. Goals are inspiring and need to be set constantly. When you stop setting goals, you are no longer going to be motivated to accomplish anything.

Respect and trust are additionally 2 other things you need to think about. Individuals have to be trusted and appreciated, and when they understand they have these 2 things from you, they are going to react to you in a better way. If you are attempting to inspire others, you want to give individuals respect and trust since they are going to wish to do things for you.

Constructive criticism is additionally really essential for making the most of motivation. If you are attempting to motivate others, you ought to constantly be constructive and not harmful. Beating somebody down is not going to help them end up being inspired, yet it may make the circumstance worse.

When you offer constructive criticism, you could still see the favorable result of the situation and you can additionally assist individuals in finding positive ways to fix circumstances. This includes you as well. Never ever beat yourself up. Every day, you want to bring positive reinforcement and additionally constructive criticism. Do not be tough on yourself. Keep in mind, life is harder for somebody else somewhere.

Make life enjoyable. When you work on projects at work and in your private life, you want to discover the fun in all of the procedures. Making things enjoyable can aid to motivate others who are having a difficult time. If your work does not feel like work, you are going to enjoy it a lot more. If your employees lack motivation, then make it an enjoyable and positive environment. This is going to result in outstanding outcomes with the staff instead of issues with hostility.

Communication is one more way to stay motivated and to inspire others. You want to be certain all communication lines are open and that there is never a disconnect. If there are any prospective issues which might develop, you want to be familiar with all the things which might occur. The more mindful you are of problems that might emerge, the less serious it appears when they take place. Awareness can additionally help you to stop things from happening as well.

Stimulation is very important as well. Make sure every day you practice something which is stimulating. Stimulation is good for the brain and to stay motivated. If you do the identical thing each day, you are going to end up being bored, find it difficult to reach goals, and lack motivation. Make certain you produce a stimulating environment for yourself or simply mix things up a little. All you need to do is change things up a little. It could assist you to be passionate and additionally have the chance to see the big picture in life as well.

Improvements are essential. Something you have to add to your motivational routine is to demand improvements. As you practice your motivational strategies you could discover ways to enhance your mindset and how you do things. You could discover particular areas which you can make better. As you see these areas you could produce a focal point and establish objectives too. This is going to aid in keeping you motivated to pursue these goals.

Striving for improvement is an outstanding method to stay clear of stagnation. When individuals improve or you improve do not hesitate to raise the bar. This assists individuals to excel even further beyond what you or others may have thought you were capable of.

You ought to additionally produce opportunities for you or others to take full advantage of motivation. If you do not see an opportunity to advance, then you want to discover one. This implies developing an opportunity. This implies that you could end up being motivated when you see the possibilities in things which you could attain. This additionally suggests that you have to provide or create opportunities for workers too. When you understand how your hard work can really create a payoff, you are going to be more inspired.

Motivation works excellent when there is a possibility sitting before of somebody.

One more thing to consider is being imaginative. When you work on your motivational strategies each day, make sure you are imaginative. Never ever hesitate to utilize your imaginative side. If you are accustomed to getting shot down when you are imaginative, disregard these things. It is healthy to be imaginative. Encourage imagination in others as well. Certain individuals have a lot they could teach you when you show them you have an interest in seeing their imaginative side.

Conclusion

If you discover that you are having a difficult time being motivated to make it through the day or particular projects regularly, there are particular things you may do. Motivation consists of a mix of behaviors, so you could feel the spark to achieve particular goals and other things.

If you are motivated, you have the zest you require to make it through anything. There are numerous things you want to do if you lack motivation. A number of the things you could practice every day consist of how you think. Positive thinking is among the most significant things you want to practice. Whenever you feel negative about something, you want to pinch yourself and remember that you are working on motivation. Positive thinking constantly is going to aid you in seeing the good in all the things.

Individuals you socialize with have a huge effect on you even if you do not think they do. When you surround yourself with positive and inspired individuals, you are going to feel the same way each day. The ideal thing you could do for you is to spend time around individuals who are encouraging and believe in your goals. Individuals who increase your spirit and your mindset are the ideal individuals you could have in your life. They are going to help generate the motivation you require to meet goals and reach higher daily.

Daily motivational methods have to be carried out so as to feel terrific about attaining goals. As you start working toward motivating yourself, you may discover a few of these approaches tough to carry out. You may have to develop a list of the important things you have to do. These things might not come quickly to you, and you are going to need to work hard towards all of these goals. Do not worry. After time, you are going to discover that your motivational methods are going to come naturally, and you are no longer going to have to even try. You are going to be a positive and motivated individual that many people like to be around too.

I hope that you enjoyed reading through this book and that you have found it useful. If you want to share your thoughts on this book, you can do so by leaving a review on the Amazon page. Have a great rest of the day.